AF871676

36 Ways Your Bookkeeper Steals From You

Uncovering Bookkeeping Fraud:

A Guide for Small Business Owners

Charlie Montgomery

ISBN: 9798951549082

This book is intended for general informational and educational purposes only. It reflects the author's personal experience and opinions gained over decades of bookkeeping and business consulting work, and is not intended as legal, accounting, investigative, or financial advice.

Every business situation is different. If you suspect fraud, theft, or financial misconduct in your organization, you should consult a licensed CPA, forensic accountant, attorney, or law enforcement professional before taking action, particularly before confronting an employee or making decisions that could carry legal consequences.

The author and publisher make no guarantees regarding the outcomes of applying the strategies described in this book and disclaim any liability for losses or damages, direct or indirect, arising from the use of this information.

INTRODUCTION

For forty-five years, my consulting business with small businesses was built on referrals. Most of the time, the referral included the accounting/bookkeeping function, either as a part of the requested duties or as a trainer for an existing or new bookkeeper.

One of the services I provided was complete management for a small business that might be struggling or even almost at the point of bankruptcy. This type of consulting always involved isolating why the business was in trouble, and I found there were about a dozen repetitive reasons why a business was not succeeding.

The three most common issues I encountered were:

1. The owner would not structure their time and mental focus on the part of the business that brought in money. This included the owner performing jobs in the company that should have been funneled to others. For instance: the owner was not focused on growing the business; instead, the owner used their time to do simple bookkeeping. One cannot do more than time allows, and I found these owners had become exhausted from the constant drain of top-line ownership issues and would instead focus on duties that were easier and less stressful, such as the bookkeeping, cleaning the warehouse, or rearranging the boxes in the storeroom.
2. Since the advent of the internet in the early 1990s, the availability of information has blossomed. Market trends change faster, and buyers sway and change sometimes with little notice. I have seen instances where a company's marketplace has changed, and the owner of the company has not kept up with the needs of their clients. This led clients to be siphoned off by other providers who offered new and fresh, and maybe better, options.

3. And to the point of this book, I have seen many examples where an employee had figured out how to siphon cash out of the business. I saw theft through.
    - Stealing inventory, where an employee turned around and re-sold the inventory to another competing company.
    - An employee used the company inventory to work independently, redirecting company clients to an off-the-books situation.
    - At a retail location where an employee was pocketing customers' cash payments.
    - At a food establishment/bar where the server was giving free food to friends and not even ringing up the sales at all.
    - But most often, I discovered bookkeepers who had found ways to drain cash from their employers through a variety (and sometimes, very smart) ways using the company's financial systems.

Most of the time, the cash drain was so gradual that a busy company owner didn't notice the change in his business for months and sometimes years.

Theft by a bookkeeper is a really tough subject to discuss, yet theft by a bookkeeper is much more prevalent than most business owners realize or care to admit. This is an underreported crime that is very costly to businesses and can be especially devastating to small businesses. The results of the thefts are that raises cannot be given to employees, assets cannot be purchased, and sometimes businesses must declare bankruptcy. In all cases, the owners of the companies who have experienced the thefts do not get a full return on their investment in cash, assets, and personal blood, sweat, and tears.

These are pretty strong statements.

I stand by the statements because of my experiences with clients who had pickpocket bookkeepers. Some of these bookkeepers I discovered, and there were some situations where the clients already knew something was wrong with their company cash flow.

I'm Charlie Montgomery, a full-charge bookkeeper and business advisor with more than 45 years of experience specializing in consulting with small business owners. These are some of my life's work:

- Most importantly for this guide, my specialty with accounting clients has been those companies for which tax professionals have refused to prepare a tax return because the bookkeeping records were so inadequate or inaccurate. I have taken as many as seven years of records from a client, unraveled the information, cleaned up the books, and re-submitted them to a tax preparer for tax returns. CPAs referred all these clients to me, and some of these clients are the ones I reference in this book.

In addition, I have

- Consulted with well over 100 clients in a variety of types of businesses, such as real estate, residential and commercial rental properties, large beauty salon spa owners, many manufacturing entities, retail locations, various types of construction companies, and assisted living facilities.
- Managed over 830 apartments in 15 locations when I was 26, with a staff of 115 persons, including painters, plumbers, electricians, carpenters, and landscaping.
- Owned and operated a large recruiting firm managing employment placements on a national scale.
- Was a partner in a payroll servicing company in the 1990s that processed over $26 million in payroll a year in several states. This gave me extensive knowledge of workers' compensation management, safety management, hiring/firing practices, and unemployment claim response.
- Managed a 50,000 sq foot hazardous chemical warehouse and was licensed for Level A hazardous response. I taught hazardous response to many law enforcement agencies.

- Was the emergency manager and safety manager for a large county in Texas on the border of Mexico, with a staff of six safety engineers to monitor 92 locations. Implemented the county emergency operations center, gathered and trained staff for response during hurricanes, tornadoes, and other emergencies. Wrote the first-ever county emergency plan, which was in effect for many years.
- During the initial COVID pandemic, I carefully assisted many small business owners in successfully filing for the PPP (Paycheck Protection Program) forgivable loans, ensuring compliance with Federal regulations and with each owner receiving 100% forgiveness.

This tutorial details my personal consulting experiences in assisting company owners who fell victim to their trusted employee stealing through bookkeeping procedures.

I specifically designed this business guide for small- to mid-sized business owners for self-education on how to investigate their bookkeeping systems if they suspect their cash flow is being stolen by their bookkeeper.

If you have purchased this educational guide, you are concerned for your company's future. So, we are going to get right down to what to look for in your company's bookkeeping system.

This guide will give you the tools you need to determine if your bookkeeper is trustworthy. If the bookkeeper is a pickpocket, this tool has the potential to discover theft and save the business owner thousands of dollars.

Thirty-five (35) examples used in ***36 Ways Your Bookkeeper Steals From You*** are from my **REAL WORLD EXPERIENCE**. The last example in the Payroll section was experienced by a CPA who related the story to me. I thought it was so innovative it deserved a place in my book.

The events I have personally witnessed while working with my clients over the last 45 years ended up with the owners of the companies paying for me to clean up their financial records and to find out exactly how much cash was taken.

The book is segmented based on the portion of the bookkeeping system the bookkeeper may target. For instance: accounts payable access points are listed together, accounts receivable access points are listed together, etc. This allows the business owner to thoroughly investigate one piece of their bookkeeping system at a time.

If you are questioning the accuracy of your cash flow, I strongly advise an investigation throughout your financial systems.

Only a few of the company owners pressed charges.

Good luck and have fun being a Pickpocket Investigator!!

Table of Contents

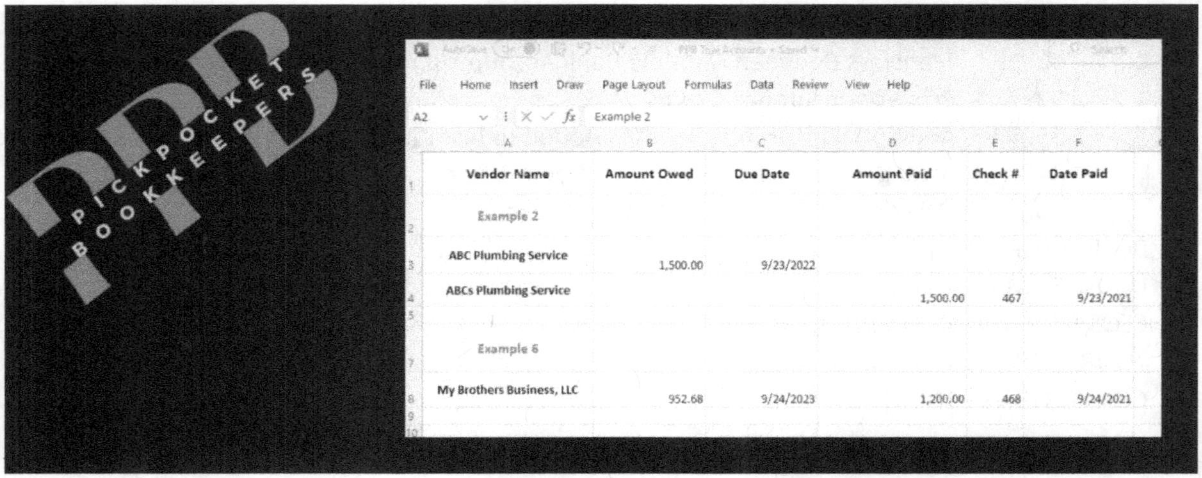

Vendor Name	Amount Owed	Due Date	Amount Paid	Check #	Date Paid
Example 2					
ABC Plumbing Service	1,500.00	9/23/2022			
ABCs Plumbing Service			1,500.00	467	9/23/2021
Example 6					
My Brothers Business, LLC	952.68	9/24/2023	1,200.00	468	9/24/2021

THEFT THROUGH ACCOUNTS PAYABLE

The part of the bookkeeping system where you pay for goods and/or services.

The bookkeeper misuses the bookkeeping system and colludes with an external party by writing checks to a bogus vendor more often than services are provided to the company.

This is when the bookkeeper introduces a vendor as someone they know. The business owner may or may not ever meet the vendor, trusting the bookkeeper to manage their financial systems. This will probably not be done right away – the bookkeeper needs to build trust with the company owner first.

Theft can be especially easy for the bookkeeper when the owner has granted check-signing authority. Even though the company owner might review the checks, it is easy to slip one or two bogus checks into a stack of checks.

The timing of the presentation of the checks to be signed is critical to the success of these scams. The busier the company owner is, the better. Many times, the owner will just sign the checks and promise to review the bills later. "Later" may come months later, and by then thousands may have been siphoned out of the company.

There are eight scenarios for accounts payable, all involving a friend, brother, sister, mother, maybe even the bookkeeper his/herself, etc., who receives the check. I have seen this with mothers who supposedly provided janitorial services, an uncle who supposedly did landscaping, a brother who supposedly serviced the company trucks, etc.

1. Extra checks written for services not performed.

In the beginning, the bookkeeper writes valid checks in the new vendor's own personal name for services actually performed.

The company owner may pay attention for a couple of months to verify that the work was actually done, then the business gets busy, the level of trust is higher, and the business owner ceases to verify that each and every service was performed. The bookkeeper presents the bills and the checks to be signed at a point when the business owner is extremely busy and ready to leave the office. All the checks are signed in less than five minutes.

The bookkeeper has added a bogus check in the middle of the stack, and the business owner never notices the bogus bill and check. The colluding person might get an extra check or two every three months or so, and the business owner has lost track of when the person was last paid for services.

It is much easier to cash a check in your own name than in a company name. After having been scammed this way, one of my clients would no longer write vendor checks in individual people's names – he insisted each individual file for and receive a D/B/A certificate from the county. This means the person receiving the check will have to have a corresponding bank account in the D/B/A name. While this does not stop theft completely, it certainly is a deterrent because most thieves are essentially lazy and want to find the path of least resistance.

2. Checks Written to a Bogus Vendor OR With a Bogus Date

The bookkeeper writes checks to a company name that looks really close to one of the company's major vendors. For instance, Jones Window Washing, Inc., would be duplicated as Jones Windows.

The colluding person files a D/B/A in the closely related name and actually gets a bank account. The business owner is accustomed to seeing repetitive vendor checks, and since the name is so similar, the owner doesn't pick up the difference.

Checks are paid for services never rendered. If the bank calls to verify the check, the bookkeeper verifies the bank. The owner might even verify the check because the company name is so close.

Also, these "look-alike" vendor checks are often written with a date that is a prior bookkeeping year. This makes the checks much harder to find, because when you pull the Vendor Check Detail report, these checks will not pull on your report. For instance, if you are in the 2023 bookkeeping year, the check might be written for 2021 and posted to a balance sheet account. See Section 7 of this document. Also see the Video Presentation for Accounts Receivable.

I had a client whose bookkeeper had set up no less than three duplicated companies for this system. The client lost $60,000 before he contracted with me to investigate his accounting system.

3. Checks Written to a Vendor Different from the One Presented to the Company Owner

On a very stressful and over-filled day, the bookkeeper presents a bill for services from one of the company's long-term vendors. The company owner approves the bill, and the bookkeeper asks the company owner to "just sign this blank check and I'll get it in the mail tonight for the bill you just saw."

The bookkeeper instead writes the check to the bogus vendor, aka the colluding person mentioned above. In the bookkeeping system, the bookkeeper shows the check was written to the original valid vendor, yet the check was written to the bogus vendor. The company owner does not know there is an unpaid bill to the original vendor.

This is very easy to do in today's bookkeeping systems. The owner never would think to verify the actual checks that went through the bank to compare the vendor names.

4. Checks Written to Vendors Who Don't Call to Collect on a Timely Basis

Again, this is using a bogus vendor name and bank account to cash the checks. Here, the bookkeeper sees which vendors are careless with their own receivables, and who won't call for six or seven months to collect from you. In addition, who would the vendor call for payment? The bookkeeper.

The bookkeeper writes checks where the company owner believes he is paying one of the company's trusted vendors, most likely a vendor who performs regular services for the company and who may have been a vendor for several years.

The bookkeeper actually writes the checks in the company bookkeeping system; the owner signs the checks and goes on their merry way.

The bookkeeper then cashes the checks in the bogus bank account and **deletes** the checks from the bookkeeping system. This means the Accounts Payable in the bookkeeping system is accurate, but the bank reconciliation will be off.

This goes on for months. The company owner doesn't require an accounts payable monthly register to notice the bills are not being paid. The company owner also ceases to receive the documentation on bank reconciliation on a monthly basis.

Another twist is when the bookkeeper deletes the original check, processes a check for the same amount in the accounting system, and posts it to the balance sheet chart of accounts. Most company owners do not review their balance sheet accounts as closely as their Profit & Loss accounts, and this can slide by for months. This corrects the accounts payable subledger, allows for a bank reconciliation, and effectively buries the transaction.

The bookkeeper usually quits just as the business owner gets suspicious and either starts asking for many more specific reports or hires someone like me to review the accounting.

I cleaned up a set of books behind a bookkeeper that did this with 10 vendors in a company. She took approximately $80,000.00 in three years. The owner filed charges, but she had moved out of state, and I don't know that they ever caught her. The owner actually had to make partial restitution to his vendors to keep his business afloat.

5. **Vendor Invoices are Paid Twice, and the bookkeeper pockets the duplicate payment.**

A pickpocket bookkeeper can write a check for a bill your company paid three weeks ago, get the check signed with the rest of the weekly checks, and the company owner doesn't pick up on the duplication. Then the bookkeeper changes the check number and possibly the name on the check in the computer so you can't find the duplicated payments.

In this type of theft, the company owner does not review each week the bills that are being paid. The owner must ask for random reports by vendor to see an overview of vendor payments. Also, the owner should ask for a monthly check register and should review three months' check registers for reference to pick up duplications.

6. **Checks are written for more than the amount billed to your company.**

This occurs when you buy from the bookkeeper's family member or personal partner or long-term fellow thief.

I found one bookkeeper who was colluding with a vendor who billed, for instance, $1,000 for services. The bookkeeper, who was dating the vendor, had the vendor send in bills for more than the amount quoted, for instance, $1,200. When the bookkeeper gave the business owner the checks to sign, sure enough, there would be a matching invoice for $1,200.

The bookkeeper then cashed the check and pocketed the extra $200 as a kickback for giving the vendor the business in the first place.

The original invoice for $1,000 was filed in the filing system, so if the owner wanted to see a past amount that was billed, no problem. The owner never thought to check whether the amount paid matched what was filed in the filing system.

This scenario is easy to do, because time passes, and the details of each transaction become blurred.

Have a policy that your purchases cannot be from any family member of the bookkeeper. Nepotism is banned in most firms for this very reason.

Make sure the bills are given to you along with the checks to sign and make sure the amounts match. **LOOK at them** to see if you are paying too much for the services/products. If you ever catch just one bill being paid at a higher rate, immediately find help from an outside accounting professional to review everything in your accounting system. This could very well be the tip of the iceberg, and the sooner you find the issues, the more money you can retain.

7. Posting vendor payments to a Balance Sheet account – never affecting the Profit and Loss.

Many companies pay bonuses based on company profitability, which means the Profit and Loss report. Bonuses can be quarterly or annually.

Many business owners are familiar with a form called "Profit and Loss." However, many business owners have no idea something exists named a "Balance Sheet."

How this plays out is the pickpocket bookkeeper sets up a Balance Sheet account and posts bogus payments to the colluding person to this Balance Sheet account instead of to the Profit and Loss accounts. The payment escapes the owner's attention because the owner only looks at the Profit and Loss, not the Balance Sheet. The payment never affects the Profit and Loss, which is what the bookkeeper's bonus is based upon.

This way of posting is a double whammy to the business owner. Not only is his cash account draining out, but also the bookkeeper is building up her quarterly or year-end bonus amount.

Bonuses are often paid at the end of the four quarterly periods or the end of the year. When the end of the bookkeeping year happens on December 31, the company books are not usually turned over to the CPA until sometime in February or even March. During this time lag, the bookkeeper uses bogus reports to get a large bonus, and sometimes the DAY the books are turned over to the CPA, the bookkeeper quits. The owner is not only out the bonus, but the cash has been drained out of the company.

The worst example I saw was when a bookkeeper received a $20,000 bonus and had not actually paid the payroll taxes. The employer owed $75,000 to the IRS plus was out the bonus, which was significant. The bookkeeper quit the job in the middle of January before the books went to the CPA.

8. Key Contractor (family members) taking monies, not reported on 1099

This happens when family members are in business together.

If the bank balance doesn't get reconciled, who knows who received a check? There is no absolute report without reconciliations of all accounts, including all credit card accounts. These credit card accounts should reconcile just like the bank accounts.

An unauthorized check written to a family member may go unnoticed for several months, especially if the family member has access to a checkbook and hand-writes the checks. I have seen family members write themselves unauthorized checks without their partners/other family members knowing until much later. The most egregious situation I witnessed was a son who wrote himself a $75,000 check when his dad unexpectedly was admitted to a hospital for a serious illness. The family was in an uproar, the dad was not around to monitor the cash flow, and the son took advantage.

Family members often work "contract." This is a bad decision to start with because most "contract workers" are supposed to charge and pay sales tax, at least in the State of Texas. If you have never been through a sales tax audit and are paying family members "contract," you are extremely lucky you have not had an audit. These audits are very expensive, and once triggered, the auditing agency has the option to go back several years. I recently had a client audited for three years; he paid over $20,000 in sales tax.

If these persons were not family, the business owners would file theft charges. However, because they are family, most times nothing is done. As a matter of fact, often the offending family member retains banking privileges and continues the theft for a period of time, often years.

The final issue with family members being "contract" workers is that a 1099 is not prepared at the end of the year. This means the company cannot claim the payment as part of business expenses on their corporate tax return.

One of the CPAs I coordinated with on the above situation with the $75,000 check refused to do the corporate tax return without a 1099 being issued to the son. This created quite an unhappy son, because he was forced to pay income tax on the $75,000.

DEFENSE FOR ACCOUNTS PAYABLE SITUATIONS

- **NEVER** have the bookkeeper have signing authority on the checks.
- Organize your office so that you get checks on Thursday night, and you issue checks once a week on Friday. This provides a clear overview of what is being paid.
- Insist that repetitive checks come to you on a schedule each month: rent on the first Friday, utilities maybe on the third Friday, etc.
- LOOK at the checks as you sign them and compare the bill to the check amount. Don't just flip through doing the signatures, trusting that the checks are accurate.
- Insist that the bills you received from the vendor be attached to each check. READ them.
- Insist on seeing the Balance Sheet each month. Know what goes on the balance sheet, know which accounts should have postings during the year, know how to recognize suspicious postings, and have an outside third-party person look at your books on a regular basis.

- Be clear to the bookkeeper that their postings will be reviewed when you hire that person.
- Insist on an Accounts Payable Summary Report pulled directly from your bookkeeping program, not an Excel spreadsheet (which can be manipulated by the bookkeeper). Keep the reports in a file and compare three months at a time.
- As part of your year-end procedures, send out questionnaires to your top fifteen vendors requesting lists of "open" (unpaid) bills. I have clients that require this procedure two times a year. Have the answers sent to you personally at a different address, like a post office box only you can access.
- Once a month, ask for reports for the core vendors showing current year-to-date amounts and the corresponding dates for last year. Check to see if your vendors are getting paid steadily more than last year's totals.
- Ask for a vendor list once a year. Look for repetitive vendor names. Look for names you do not recognize.

THEFT THROUGH PETTY CASH

Can you buy a "petty cash" at Wal-Mart?

Do you have one of those in your own refrigerator?

A petty cash check should not be written to "petty cash." It should have a payee for the company owner's name under a special vendor name "John Smith Petty Cash."

A bookkeeper writing checks to petty cash translates to me that someone is taking cash out of the business. Someone has to go to the bank and get cash for the check, and often the business owner delegates that to the bookkeeper; it's such a minor duty.

NOTE: One of the things I see in my consulting is business owners and/or key employees write a check for Petty Cash, planning on turning in the receipts later. Over time, this becomes just another cash cow, especially for a thief.

NOTE: And, by the way, **MAKE SURE** if you take cash out for "petty cash" that check is NOT written to your name as the corporate owner under the same vendor name you use for actual reimbursements of what you, as the owner, have paid out of your own money – these are a different classification of payment.

Set up two vendor names, one for "John Smith Reimbursements" and the other for "John Smith Petty Cash." That way, if you are audited, the auditor can quickly differentiate what the checks were for, which will limit your IRS audit – always a good thing.

9. Petty Cash is not Set Up Correctly in the Bookkeeping System, and therefore is never really reconciled. There is no accountability by the bookkeeper, and unauthorized expenses are charged.

Petty Cash in a business bookkeeping system should be set up as a "credit card" in your accounting system and reconciled just like any other credit card account. This will mean that there must be written documentation for each payment made, just like any other transaction. Receipts should be filed in a file folder with an Excel spreadsheet itemizing how the check was posted in the bookkeeping system. IRS looks very closely at transactions to "Petty Cash."

If the owner of the business requires petty cash to be set up just like a credit card in the bookkeeping system, the bookkeeper will be required to reconcile it just as any other bank account. And there should be a firm rule that no NEW check will be written without the receipts turned in for the LAST check.

There should be a reconciliation report every month just like the other credit card reconciliation reports.

Petty cash accounts are an easy way for a bookkeeper to take out an extra couple of hundred dollars a month. The charges that are generally turned in are for gasoline (when the company has company-owned vehicles), mileage, maintenance charges on a vehicle (like a car battery), travel expenses, office supplies (this is how school supplies get buried). I have found personal phone bills, credit cards, even car payments posted to a company's petty cash account.

When I go into a client, the first place I look is in petty cash, and I require the documentation to match exactly what is posted in the accounting system.

10. Petty Cash / Expense Reimbursement is Inflated

This is where the bookkeeper will take a gas receipt, which is an authorized expense, maybe by a company delivery person, and the receipt might be for $30.00. The bookkeeper posts the receipt as $35.00 and takes the extra $5.00 for themselves. This may seem like a petty amount, but you multiply this transaction by maybe 30 transactions a month, and over a period of a year you will have a significant amount of money siphoned off the company.

Usually, the amounts are kept pretty small so as to avoid any real notice. Over time, however, this can add up to a nice little unauthorized raise for the bookkeeper.

How the bookkeeper gets away with this is that the owner is never checking the receipts against the accounting system.

Pickpocket bookkeepers are petty thieves. They will have no idea how much money they are taking over a long period of time. They just knew they needed $5.00 for gas that day and they found a way to get it.

CASE STUDY:

In reviewing one client's records, I found checks to "Petty Cash" were being processed every couple of weeks. I asked the business owner who reviewed the Petty Cash reimbursements and was told it was the trusted bookkeeper who prepared the reports and wrote out the checks. The business owner never really reviewed the documentation; he just signed the checks.

I noticed the bookkeeper had a new purse, and it looked like it was a designer brand. Now, I am not an expert on designer purses, so I asked her, "That's a great purse. Where did you purchase it?"

"Down in the manufacturer's district. I'm sure it's a knock-off, but I liked it."

At lunch, I asked the bookkeeper to go and pick up lunch for us. I watched as she left the building to go to her car. Funny – it was a late-model KIA.

When she came back, I asked her if she liked her KIA; I was shopping for a new car. She extolled the virtues of all the bells and whistles on her top-of-the-line car. I asked her how much her payment was and how much she had to put down on it. “I didn’t have much of a down payment,” she gleefully told me, “I only had to put $5,000 down on the car, and that was covered by my trade-in, and my payment is ONLY $675 a month.”

Then I asked her about her kids – everyone likes to talk about their kids. She had three, all in middle school and high school. I asked her how she kept up with her kids while she was at work, that I had had a lot of trouble doing that when I was raising my own child. She said, “They all have cell phones, and I have the tracking system on the phone.”

FIVE phones in that family.

Then I asked if her kids were in extracurricular activities. Sure enough, they were. Now, I have clients that moan and groan about how much time and money extracurricular activities cost for their kids.

Get the picture? This bookkeeper was living way above the salary level of her job.

So that afternoon, I left her office at 5:00. The owner and I went to have coffee, and at 6:30 I was back at the office starting to do my real work. By midnight, in one year’s transactions, I had identified where she had possibly taken $35,000 from the company in various unauthorized transactions – petty cash, duplicate vendors, extra payroll checks. You name it, she did it.

The owner and I didn’t say a word. Not yet.

The next night I came back and started pulling records, invoices, bills, and other documentation. By midnight, I had the paperwork ready to take to the police. Law enforcement accepted the case three days later, and the bookkeeper was arrested at work.

It is important to bide your time until you have a final word on what has been going on. The documentation has to be clear and understandable so law enforcement will accept the case.

Also, at the time you fire the person, you want to be able to change all passwords (accounting system, banking, vendors, online payments), collect all keys, get all credit cards the person may be carrying, and change the locks on the doors. This takes some coordination.

DEFENSE FOR PETTY CASH SITUATIONS

- The company owner should require petty cash be reconciled just like any other bank account.
- The owner of the company should be the only one to sign the petty cash/reimbursement check after reviewing all the items on the reconciliation report. If possible, be sure it's only the company owner who cashes the check. I have seen owners look at reports I have pulled and not be familiar with half of the petty cash checks that were written because they had authorized the bookkeeper to handle the reimbursement all the way through cashing the check.
- Set up rigid requirements for administering petty cash and expense reimbursements. Require all expenses to be paid by regular check, deal very little with cash, and use a credit card or debit card.
- Ask the bookkeeper to pull reports for the vendor "John Smith Petty Cash." Look at the totals and see if one or two payments are especially high; ask for the detailed Excel spreadsheet and the accompanying receipts.
- **LOOK** at the receipts every month, religiously!

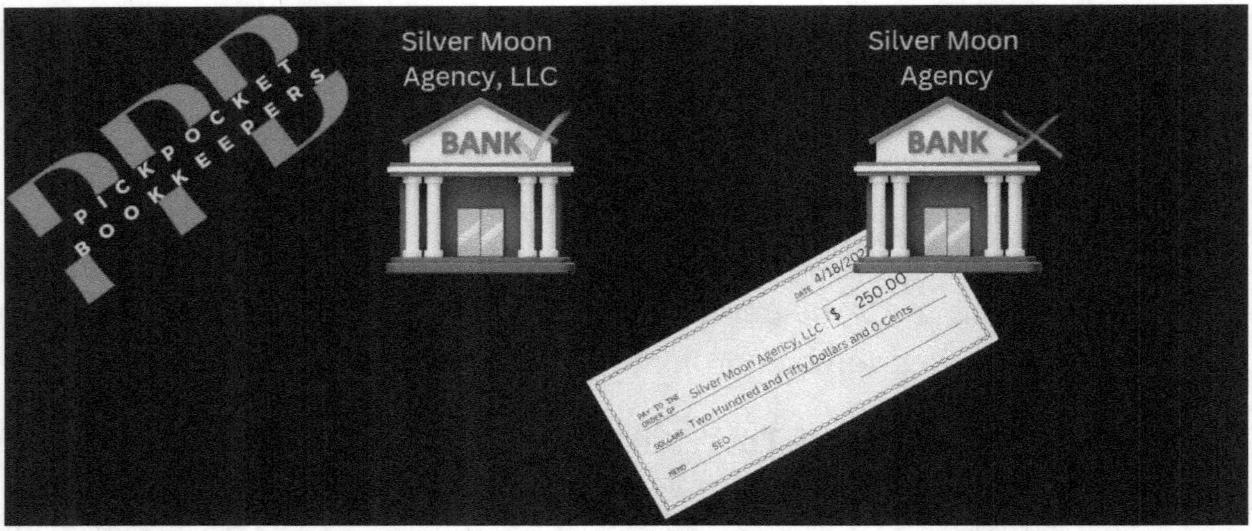

THEFT THROUGH ACCOUNTS RECEIVABLE

The part of the bookkeeping system where clients pay your company.

The setup to all these situations is the bookkeeper and a colluding person set up a DBA and a bogus bank account at a secondary bank under a name that is almost exactly like your company's name. They might just leave off "Inc" or "LLC."

The bookkeeper will have some closely related person on the bank's Corporate Resolution as "Owner" or "President" to open the account.

I recently saw this exact scenario – it was her boyfriend. The pickpocket bookkeeper even notarized the boyfriend's signature on the Bank Resolution as the President of the corporation.

11. Redirecting Client Payments to the Bogus Bank Account

In this scenario, client invoices were paid by checks to the company. The accounting system is satisfied as far as accounts receivable is concerned.

But here's the problem.

The bookkeeper never tells the company owner the check arrived for this customer.

The bookkeeper waits until Friday afternoon to deposit the check into the bogus business account, because the business owner is not as focused on work on the weekends and doesn't check the bank balance as often. There is more of a chance the check will not activate a red flag, because the payee on the check is so close to the name on the bogus bank account, the bank clerk doesn't pick up any difference, and neither will the company owner. It works.

In the bookkeeping system, the bookkeeper issues a credit to the original client and the accounts receivable report balances.

The bookkeeper leaves unexpectedly early (after all, it's Friday) and weekly reports don't get prepared. By Monday, the business owner had forgotten to insist on the weekly reports. By the next week, there is a whole new set of circumstances for the business owner to deal with, and they don't remember that a few checks came in from clients, and by the way, where are those checks posted?

The bookkeeper knows all these habits and schedules and is counting on all these systems to play out in their favor. Most often, it does.

12. Multiple or Incorrect Invoices Sent to Customers

I have seen several cases of this. The scenario process is like this:

Multiple invoices are sent to a customer, maybe for different amounts and slightly different services, and both scenarios involved a larger client with multiple accounts payable clerks.

The customer's bookkeeping department goes ahead and pays both invoices by check.

When the second check arrived, the receipt for the second invoice was handmade (off the books), thereby satisfying the customer's systems.

The second check was cashed through a check-cashing place. The second invoice was then canceled and disappeared completely from the bookkeeping system. The only record of the receipt of funds was the receipt for payment sent to the customer that was created in Excel and was not entered at all in the company's accounting software.

At first, it seemed like the bookkeeper did small amounts, and when a customer would complain (which doesn't always happen), the bookkeeper would just issue a refund check (remember, small amounts) and tell the owner it was for overpayment.

The business owner didn't recognize the number of times it had happened and, after a while, didn't even look, because there was always an explanation.

Later, after the bookkeeper quit, the owner started getting the questions that the bookkeeper kept from him. In order to keep his customer base, the owner had to refund several customers to the tune of about $5,000 each.

I had a client who discovered his minority partner was stealing from him in multiple ways. One of the ways was duplicated billing, in the amount of $100,000 through credit card processing. The customer and my client's firm had done business for many years, and believe it or not, the minority partner had their credit card number to do billing and collections.

The customer picked up the extra $100,000 payment; the minority partner told them there had been a glitch with the credit card processing company. The minority partner made a deal with the customer to issue credits for future business until the $100,000 was accounted for, NEVER TELLING the majority partner. All the majority partner could see was that, for some mysterious reason, the receivables were dropping.

After the majority partner figured out the minority partner was stealing from the company, he contacted me. I told him to work with receivables first, because income was critical. He found out through his calls that the client still was owed $50,000 and was expecting credits for future business. Needless to say, not only was he surprised, but he was truly angry that his supposedly long-term partner had made off with another $100,000.

13. The bookkeeper pockets cash taken for payment from clients.

This is a variation on the above but having to do with taking cash: the bookkeeper was taking in the cash, issuing the receipt to the customer, then voiding both the invoice and the receipt in the bookkeeping system and pocketing the cash.

After I found this in one of my clients' bookkeeping systems and asked the business owner about what I saw was happening, the business owner indicated they had no clue how much the bookkeeper took – the only thing that might be a clue was the owner was missing about $10,000 in inventory at the end of the year.

14. The accounts receivable clerk inflated charges billed to clients to increase quarterly bonuses.

This scenario was between two large national entities.

The bookkeeper for the service provider added fraudulent (elevated) charges to a customer's invoices for only four months. The customer paid the invoices on time. Someone in the customer's accounting department noticed that the current year's invoices totaled more than the same period last year. Yet, the agreed-upon pricing was the same, and the number of invoices was approximately equal. An audit was done at the customer level, and the service provider had to return more than $200,000 to the well-valued customer.

The reason the bookkeeper did this?

The whole office staff was on a quarterly bonus system based on production. Business had slowed down somewhat, and the bookkeeper took it upon herself to pad the invoices in order to keep bonuses high. So, the service provider not only had to return money to the customer, but the estimated elevated bonuses paid were about $30,000 to several people, and the business owner did not see a way to rescind the bonuses.

DEFENSE FOR ACCOUNTS RECEIVABLE SITUATIONS

- Scenarios 11 and 12 above: Have the bookkeeper pull a monthly list of invoices which shows the customer's name and invoice amount, sorted by customer name. Keep the report. Then every six months, have the bookkeeper pull the report for the current six months. Compare the reports. If something is missing, start investigating.
- Scenario 13 above: Review customer invoices on a monthly basis in your bookkeeping system. Look for anything that seems unusual. Ask the bookkeeper to provide backup to any questionable invoice(s). Also, compare the previous years' billing totals to the current year's totals. Look for any gross increase, using your knowledge of the customer activity.
- Scenario 14 above: Periodically pull sales reports by customer, comparing the current quarter or year with the previous year's corresponding time period. Look for any gross change up or down, using your knowledge of what is happening in the marketplace and with your customers.

THEFT THROUGH USE OF COMPANY CREDIT CARDS

15. Bookkeeper uses the business credit cards as if they were the bookkeeper's private cards.

It is common for business owners to have an office supply store credit card or general supply account that the bookkeeper has freedom to use. This is for ease of ordering repetitive supplies such as paper, pens, tape, etc.

The only problem is supply stores **ALSO** sell water, beverages, candy, food, paper towels, toilet paper, school supplies, laptops, printers, and many other desirable products. I can't tell you how many times I have been brought in to look at a company's books, and the first thing that I find is unauthorized charges on the office supply account or the company gas card.

I have found furniture, software, monitors, and computers. There are three ways the bookkeeper hides these items:

- The owner doesn't review and initial each credit card charge receipt (because, after all, it's only office supplies).
- The bookkeeper may make a payment directly to the credit card company, and the check the owner approves each month is not paying for the **COMPLETE** cost of the hidden items; **and/or**
- The bookkeeper doesn't process the **FULL** month-end balance for payment and includes only maybe a third of the bogus charge for three months. This increases the monthly check by some minimum amount, and the owner doesn't catch the increase. Three months later, the bill is

hidden in the files, and the business owner is accustomed to paying the increased minimum.

Pickpocket bookkeepers are known to use corporate vendors for personal purchases. Their answer is always: "I meant to pay that myself and accidentally paid it by company credit card instead of my personal card, and then I forgot about it." If that happens **ONCE**, start looking at everything, and maybe even pay for a forensic accountant to review everything.

CASE STUDY:

Recently I had a majority stockholder client whose minority partner was the bookkeeper. They had worked together in a firm for 15 years, bought out the business, and were partners for five years.

When the majority client received a call from the bank saying that there were bounced checks, the majority client started paying real careful attention to the books. Before then, he had depended on his long-term friend to handle all the behind-the-scenes paperwork.

The majority partner discovered a whole credit card that had been owned by the previous owner and was supposed to have been closed at the time of the sale of the business. Instead, the bookkeeper kept it open, charged over $250,000 to this credit card, and had the company pay the charges. Most of the charges were for personal items.

Needless to say, this opened Pandora's box. The minority partner was fired, I was called in to do an assessment, and we found many, many questionable items: checks written to the bookkeepers' family members, other credit card charges on the known business credit card, questionable vendor payments, you name it.

But the bogus credit card was the game-changer.

16. Hidden Payments to Staff's Personal Credit Cards and Utilities

Let us say the business has a Chase VISA card.

The bookkeeper acquires a personal Chase VISA card from the same credit card provider. Payments in the accounting system look identical.

Because you, the owner, aren't watching your money, the bookkeeper pays both cards with business money. It all looks like a payment to the same Chase VISA account. This is particularly common when the payments are made online.

At first, the payments for the bookkeeper's personal card will be small so as to go undetected, with a gradual increase in the amount of the payments. It conditions the business owner to not inquire as to why 1) there are MORE payments to the card, and 2) why the monthly total is creeping up.

A procedure that is also fairly common with pickpocket bookkeepers is to see these credit card payments posted in a group on the last day of the month. This allows the bookkeeper to pull expense reports to the **NEXT TO LAST day of the month** and avoid reporting the credit card payments to the company owner on the month-end reports. By the next month, the payments fold into Year-To-Date, and the owner doesn't catch the increase. **Watch your monthly reports for inclusive dates to the last day of each month.** Even if it goes on for only a year, this can be thousands.

CASE STUDY:

A client came to me not understanding why they weren't making more money. Business was booming, the technical staff was always booked, and their customers were paying in full and on time.

The first thing I asked the bookkeeper for was paper copies of all the credit card statements and the reconciliation reports. She informed me she did not keep any paper records of the credit card statements; everything was online.

This was a ruse. The reason she did not keep paper records was to keep the business owner from snooping in the files and looking at the actual charges. It worked.

I found that the bookkeeper had added her personal VISA charges, her Verizon charges, and her own utility bills (she transferred her services to the same providers).

The owner couldn't easily track the dollars, especially after the first couple of months of double payments. The increased costs were established as normal in the bookkeeping system. This worked for **TEN YEARS**. I estimated the trusted employee walked off with over $80,000 in personal payments alone, and I had only audited four years at that point. When I told the owner what I had found, he refused to fire the employee because she was so "integral to the daily operations of the company." I have no idea if he even talked to her about the issue.

16. Gasoline Cards, Theft Type 1

Some companies have employees that drive all the time for the company business, and instead of paying mileage, the company gives out gasoline cards. This lets the employees keep their trucks full and continue servicing clients. This is easier for the owners.

CASE STUDY:

I have a client who had a bookkeeper who was tasked with going to the bank every week, buying office supplies, and running a specific set of errands each week. Nothing else.

The client carefully calculated how much mileage the bookkeeper should have been turning in, figured out the cost at $.55 per mile (IRS current rate at that time), and gave the employee a weekly authorized budget on the card of $62.50 per week.

The first month, the second month, no problem. The owner relaxed, quit looking at the bills, and the bookkeeper paid the bill online, as usual.

Six months later, I came in to review the books (surprise!), and I found that the $62.50 had become $120 per week.

There actually was a written agreement signed between the owner and the bookkeeper for the mileage amount. When I gave the owner the information, he called the bookkeeper in for a discussion. This was against my advice, because I wanted to get more information from the accounting system in case the employee was stealing in other ways, and I would have an information source while I was looking through the system. Instead, the owner immediately called in the bookkeeper, who quit right on the spot when the owner wanted reimbursement.

After that, I continued auditing and found that wasn't the only way she was stealing from the company. The amount of loss was MUCH more. We filed charges with the local law enforcement, which took about two weeks, and by then the bookkeeper had disappeared from her last known address.

ALWAYS wait to confront an employee who is stealing in case you want to file charges so you will have access to that person with law enforcement.

In a more general sense, **MANY** times the employee adds an extra tank of gas for his wife's car or for his kid's truck on the company card.

It is VERY hard to catch this. But it can be done. All you have to do is look at the receipts for multiple charges on the same day at the same time. After all, the employee with the gas card has to be there at the same time the family car has to be there. The employee cannot give the card to the family member because the employee never knows when they will need the card for company gas.

The bookkeeper has to collude for this to happen. Meaning: They like the driver, or they are secretly dating the driver, and they keep quiet. After all, the bookkeeper is the one who is looking at the receipts and calculating the mileage costs (see below), and who is posting in the accounting system.

NOTE: Check with your human resource consultant to see if it's legal in your state to have an agreement signed by all employees who have access to company credit cards. This agreement should have the provision that if unauthorized charges are found on the card, the company has the right to deduct the unauthorized charges from the next-coming salary check.

Never hand out a final check until the company credit card has been reconciled to make sure you get reimbursement for all unauthorized charges.

On two occasions, I discovered the bookkeepers were in collusion with several employees at their companies to get kickbacks from the employees on overcharges.

17. Gasoline Cards, Theft Type 2

Some employers, specifically landscapers and the trades companies (plumbers, carpentry, handymen, electrical), issue gasoline cards to their truck drivers. This can be a good practice when employees are widespread for business reasons.

BEFORE you give out the card, do three things:

- Check with your human resources provider to have an authorization agreement that says unauthorized charges can be payroll deducted from the employee's check, with a witness on the signature part. If you use the bookkeeper as the witness and something happens, you probably won't be able to deduct from the bookkeeper's paycheck, but you can fire the bookkeeper for collusion because they knew the rules.
- Figure out how much the gas should be; this should be within $30.00. It's easy to do, even with changing gasoline costs. Ask the bookkeeper to do the calculation for you and keep a separate file with the calculations.

Employees only have so many hours they work each day, so they can only handle a certain number of on-site client calls. When you look at a six-month sampling, you will get a good average. You might have to do a year's time if you have been growing rapidly and if you have the data.

Before the company owner authorizes payment of the credit card, require the bookkeeper to attach a summary of total miles driven versus cost of gasoline.

Do a simple calculation in a template Excel spreadsheet; keep the calculation on the company owner's desktop so they can plug in different gasoline prices as they change.

A. Go back to your last six months' mileage costs.

B. Get a good average of miles per month: total miles divided by number of months. Require the employee to record on their time sheets both the beginning mileage and the ending mileage each week. You can occasionally verify this estimated mileage by reviewing invoices to clients – if there was no invoice, there was no truck servicing the client.

C. Calculation is this: (Make a form in Excel)

Estimated Miles: Average Miles / Month
Divide By: Miles per gallon for that truck (get a calculation, in WRITING)
This gives you: Number of Gallons Needed by Month
Times: Current Gas Cost Per Gallon

This gets you: Average Monthly Budget for That Truck

Option: Add a little for "extras" – overtime client calls, oil added at the pump, etc.

This gets you: The amount the employee signs for as authorized charges. This also should be approximately the amount that should be on the credit card for that truck.

This means the employee will have to have a sheet where they write down EVERY time they charge gas, so they will know when they are hitting their limit. These sheets must be turned in every month, attached to the bills from the card. You must be firm about getting these, and it should be the bookkeeper's job. **If the bookkeeper doesn't provide this, don't write the check until documentation is provided.**

18. Auto-Truck Maintenance

There are companies that have many trucks. These companies use preferred vendors for fixing the vehicles. Bookkeepers utilize their familiarity with the maintenance vendor to repair their own vehicles.

CASE STUDY

One of my clients had a bookkeeper who had her car and her son's car repaired for FIVE years on the company's money. All the charges were billed on the company credit card.

This occurred because the bookkeeper became friends with the owner of the mechanic's shop. She told him that she was authorized by the owner to order the maintenance and that she was paying the employer back out of her salary.

The shop owner never called the company owner to verify the bookkeeper's information. The bookkeeper was absolutely not authorized. The bookkeeper had told the owner there was a repetitive problem with one of the trucks, and that was why the charges climbed over time.

When you have a preferred vendor for repair and maintenance of any equipment, whether it be vehicles or other equipment, have a signed document with the vendor that says they are authorized to perform work ONLY on company-owned equipment, and if there is any question, the ONLY person who can authorize the work is the company owner. This is because this type of theft is so common that only the company owner would have the authority to authorize any repairs on any piece of equipment that is out of the norm.

19. Credit Card Refunds

This type of theft is actually quite ingenious.

This is where charges are made on a credit card, and at a later time refunds are issued to the customer. But the refunds don't go to the customer.

CASE STUDY

I had an orthodontic client who called up and said, "I'm working harder and seem to have less money. I don't know what is happening." I pulled three years' reports, looked at the statistics, and said, "Doc, something is up. You should have more cash in the bank. Keep your eyes open."

This doctor had a merchant account to process credit card payments. I was working for a CPA who reconciled his books every month, and to reconcile the merchant account would have increased his cost with the CPA by $50.00 per month. He turned down that service. The merchant account was never reconciled.

This doctor had a key employee who worked 4 days a week, 7 hours a day, for a mere $50,000. This was his trusted employee of 10 years. When she went to him for an extra day off, he gladly gave it to her. When she came to him with financial woes, he gladly advanced her salary and had her pay him back at nominal rates, no interest.

The orthodontist had a business practice: He would quote a rate to clients with the promise that if he didn't use up all the original amount, he would refund the client. The clients were happy to comply with this practice, trusting the orthodontist.

A month after he and I spoke, his credit card merchant company called his wife at home. They had been trying to contact him at work for several months, and the key employee intercepted the calls with, "He's on vacation, he's out fishing, he's out of town." Once, she called back and pretended to have a low voice to impersonate him. They figured it out and didn't talk to her. Thank goodness the credit card company had his home number from his original application for the credit card machine and the merchant account.

They had noticed that for the last three years (which is all they could audit), there had been repeated credit card refunds sent to a repetitive credit card number. The credit card company figured out the refunds were supposed to be going to other credit card accounts, based on names associated with transactions.

The key employee had been redirecting the refunds and crediting herself with the refunds, charging them off to his clients.

We only audited three years. The bookkeeper received $48,000 in refunds in three years. Remember, she had worked there for 10 years. This means the doctor wrongfully kept $48,000 of refunds from his client base.

The doctor filed charges; the trusted employee had to pay him $10,000 down and $800 per month to avoid jail.

The doctor never looked at his books. The CPA was not tasked with finding theft. The contract with the CPA required that the CPA reconcile only the operating account each month. The doctor didn't want to pay the extra each month for the CPA office to reconcile the merchant account, which is where the theft occurred. It would have been an extra $50 a month. The bookkeepers at the CPA firm privately decided the woman probably got away with another $50,000.00 that was before the audit timetable.

DEFENSE FOR USING COMPANY CREDIT CARDS:

- Know what the gasoline budgets are. Compare the budget to the actual bills. Review the bills.
- Have different gas cards for each employee, and make sure the billings are set up to print out itemized by individual gas card. It can be done. If you can't get it with your current card, change cards. Murphy's (Wal-Mart) cards do this.
- Make the bookkeeper break down the charges by truck.
- Get the gas card statements BEFORE the bill can be paid.
- Have the bookkeeper confirm that the drivers provide the forms on the first of every month.

- Have a **contract** with the mechanic's shop that says they are authorized to work **ONLY** on the vehicles listed on the contract.
- The vendor will be notified IN WRITING, signed ONLY by the owner, if additional vehicles are to be serviced.
- Put into the contract that the owner will pay you back for any unauthorized repairs should you "accidentally" pay for these repairs. The vendor won't like this, but as a small business you must have some sort of recourse.
- Credit card payments should be reconciled through a separate bank account ("Merchant Account") every month just like the operations bank account. Receipts and refunds are processed through the merchant account, which means the refunds must be recorded in the company financial system.
- Require the same reports for this account (deposits vs. payments) as are required for the general operating account. Then learn to read the credit card company forms; require the bookkeeper to reconcile that report to their bank account reports and give all reports to you at the end of each month.

Deposit

Date 7/15/23

Name Silver Moon Agency, LLC

Account Number 123456789

My Bank, LLC
1234 E West Rd.
Smalltown, USA

CASH		
CHECKS		
	425	32
	215	75
	125	63
Subtotal	766	70
Less Cash	100	00
TOTAL	666	70

THEFT THROUGH MIS-USE OF BANK DEPOSITS

20. Bookkeeper takes cash out of deposits made at bank.

This only works when a manual deposit is made at the bank. In today's world, most transactions are now processed online.

In any accounting system, there are client invoices, and payment of these invoices is called "payments," not "deposits." These payments, once made, are posted against the invoice in the accounts receivable system, notifying the business that the client no longer owes the company for the invoice. The payment applied to the invoice is the same as the invoice amount, no problem. This clears out the Accounts Receivable subledger. Good. Everything is fine. No "deposit" is made yet in the bookkeeping system, and the money has not been taken to the bank.

THEN, second step: the bookkeeper takes the deposit to the bank – the bookkeeper is happy to do this extra service, so the business owner doesn't have to do it.

On every deposit slip, there is a place at the bottom for "cash back." Look for it – it's there.

The bookkeeper takes $5, $50, $75, or other small amounts as "cash back." This makes the deposited monies less than the amount posted against the original invoice. When the deposit is made in the bookkeeping system, the "deposit" will not match the "payment."

In order to post in the bookkeeping system these little amounts of discrepancy, the bookkeeper buries the transactions for $5, $50, etc., in "maintenance," or "office supplies," or any other account that has a lot of transactions where the little bit of extra won't raise a question.

Unless the owner knows to go LOOK, there is nothing in the accounting system that flashes "**THIEF**." All the owner knows is they are working just as hard and have less cash to spend. The bookkeeper says things like, "Well, the cost of XXXX went up again."

CASE STUDY

One of my clients was a real estate broker/home builder. He had bought a large plot of land, subdivided the land, and sold the land to people who paid him monthly payments. When the land was paid off, or at least enough was paid off to qualify for a bank loan to build a home, the real estate broker would provide construction services to build the houses.

Many of these people were from medium to low-income families. They often paid in cash.

The trusted office manager would take in the cash and write a receipt out of a tri-copy receipt book.

She would then either:

1) Post a credit in the bookkeeping system to lower the Accounts Receivable subledger, and would pocket the cash, **or**
2) Post the full payment, take the cash deposit to the bank, and would not actually deposit the full amount in the bank. There is a space on every deposit slip, as well as in all accounting software programs, for "Less Cash." She might take $75, $50, $100, for herself, whatever she felt like she needed that day, and deposit the rest.

Under the second scenario, this would satisfy the Accounts Receivable subledger. The company owner could pull an accurate list of who owed him. However, when the deposit posted, the bookkeeper had to have somewhere to post the amount she took out as "Less Cash." My first clue that this was happening was an account on the Balance Sheet called "Reconciliation Discrepancies." When I investigated that account, there was about $200,000 posted to it. Over 10 years, that's how much she had taken out for cash.

This person had worked as a key employee for 10 years for the company owner. Their families had become social friends. The company owner refused to press charges and simply moved her duties to where she was not accepting land payments anymore.

DEFENSE FOR MIS-USE OF BANK DEPOSITS:

Two of the monthly reports the company owner should require are the Payments Report and the Deposits Report. These reports should equal the same amount of money.

In most companies, these two reports are easily reconciled by the bookkeeper, because most of your "deposits" come from "payments," and the few transactions that might not come through "payments" are easily recognizable. This would be "transfers" from account to account, or owner contribution – something unusual and not having anything to do with Accounts Receivable.

Therefore, if these consistently over time don't match, you have cash missing from the deposits. These two reports cannot be combined for easy comparison. You have to run these two reports separately and then compare them.

Have the bookkeeper provide these reports every month with the other required financial reports. They must compare the two amounts each month and reconcile to you the difference. If they are a thief, they will know right away that this kind of theft will be caught.

21. Deposits Never Made to the Company Bank Account

This is a critical procedure for the bookkeeper to do every end of month.

Until the bank is officially reconciled every single month (by the 15th), you don't have a set of books for the month. There is a separate function in every software for this procedure called "Reconciliation." All bank accounts, the petty cash account, and each credit card must be reconciled to the penny each month.

When payments are accepted in the Accounts Receivable module, this creates a deposit to be made at the bank.

I have seen two ways the bookkeeper gets around this system:

1. Just leaving the deposit unmade in the bookkeeping system, thereby creating a long and unreconciled list of transactions on the Reconciliation Report.

CASE STUDY

I recently found a client who had THREE PAGES of unreconciled deposits. This was a LOT of money the long-term bookkeeper stole and never reconciled the deposits.

The business owner had never educated himself to look at the reconciliation reports, and the bookkeeper was able to take for herself all the cash payments for TEN YEARS. Just from that piece of the accounting system, we calculated she was able to pocket over $150,000.

When the owner was talking to her about this situation, the bookkeeper responded with, "I thought you knew all this time; I kept giving your reports, and you never said a thing to me. And the business was doing well so I didn't think you would begrudge me making a little more."

2. The second way the bookkeeper can divert deposits is to set up a bogus bank account under almost the same name as the company operating account, at another bank. This takes premeditation and planning, because there are regulations about how someone can open a business bank account.

CASE STUDY

My client had a key employee (office manager who also was the in-house accountant). She worked for the company for many years.

The bookkeeper set up a second account in almost the same name as the operating account for the company, had a family member sign the bank resolution to open the account, actually NOTARIZED the form stating the family member was the president of the company, and began diverting payments into the bogus account instead of the company operating account. I remember one particular transaction because it was a $20,000 check from a company client who was a law firm.

When we started digging into what was happening to the cash flow, the owner picked that particular payment to track because it was such a large sum. Neither he nor I could see where the amount was deposited in the company operating account. We called the law firm's accountant, and we obtained a copy of the processed check. It clearly was not deposited in the normal operating account. That's how we found the key employee (bookkeeper) was diverting funds.

Again, the bank reconciliation for the operating account had many "open" items on the reconciliation, making the reconciliation report pages and pages long, going back YEARS. This means while there was a transaction processed through the accounting system, certain transactions never actually made it to the bank. It turned out the bookkeeper had actually been copying the first two pages of the report to turn in to the company owner at the end of every month and hiding the unreconciled items – for years.

DEFENSE FOR DEPOSITS NEVER MADE TO COMPANY BANK ACCOUNT:

Insist on the WHOLE REPORT. Don't accept anything else.

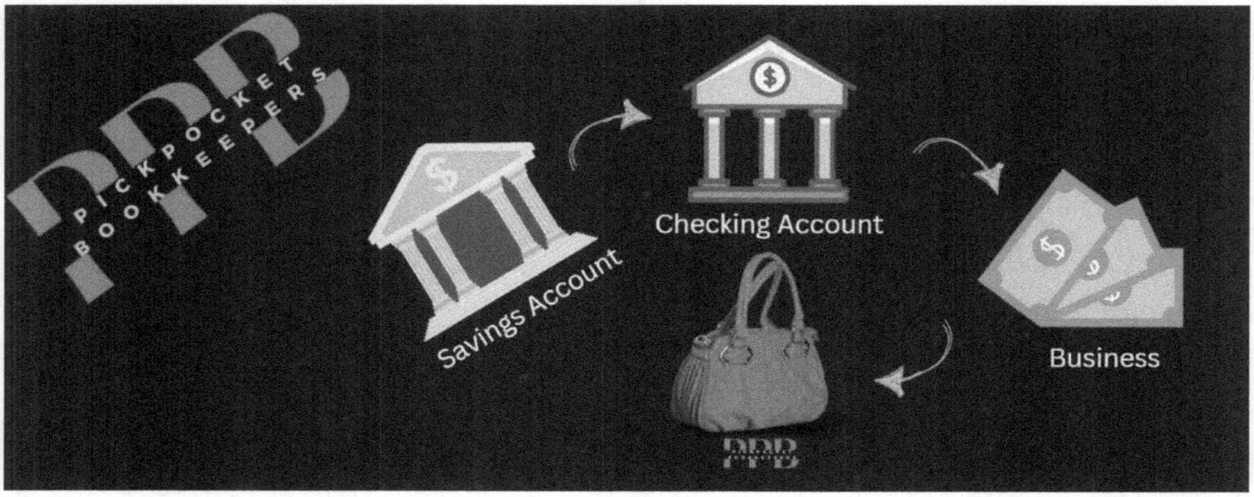

THEFT UTILIZING SAVING ACCOUNTS

One way to hide the loss of cash for a period of time is to move money from a variety of savings accounts, some of which the business owner has no idea the bookkeeper has access to. The owner may not notice this because the savings accounts are not recorded in the business bookkeeping system. This could include personal savings accounts, CD's, or investment accounts.

This is another reason the monthly reports from the bookkeeping system must include the Balance Sheet – this is where the bank balances show up.

22. Move money from a business savings account to cover a deficient operating account.

Business owners know what their operating bank balances are. They watch their operating bank balance each day online like a hawk. An extra $1,500 out of their operating account would be noticeable.

CASE STUDY

I had a client where the business owner watched the Profit & Loss very carefully and never looked at the Balance Sheet. On his bank account view, savings were on a completely different screen, and he never considered the savings amount would change.

He never noticed the savings account was depleted. He never saw the unauthorized checks going to a fraudulent vendor being posted to the Balance Sheet under an account entitled "Other Business."

The pickpocket bookkeeper was moving money from the savings account to the business account and writing fraudulent vendor checks and posting them to the Balance Sheet. The bank balance worked out, and the Profit and Loss worked out; it's just the savings account that depleted, to the tune of $15,000 in three months.

23. Move Money from Business Owner's Personal Savings Account

Business owners' personal accounts are not part of the business bookkeeping systems. A CD or other type of savings account can be at a different bank, and the owner forgets to verify that their CD or savings accounts are stable. They also sometimes forget they gave the bookkeeper access on that day they were on vacation and the owner needed money moved from the business account to the personal account on an emergency basis. However, the pickpocket bookkeeper saw an opportunity once the bookkeeper had the personal access codes.

CASE STUDY

One of my clients had a Money Market account that was personal, YET the bookkeeper had access to the money market account because the owner transferred money from his personal account to the business account when money became scarce. The personal savings account did not appear in the company books, so the account was not in any monthly report.

The bookkeeper was a thief and quit the job unexpectedly one day. A new bookkeeper was hired.
The business owner watched the Profit and Loss very carefully. He never paid attention to his personal money market account – it somehow was off his radar.

He never noticed that his Money Market had been reduced by $30,000 until the new bookkeeper just accidentally said, "....and this $100,000 Money Market. What is that?" It was supposed to be $130,000, and the business owner had to file charges on the prior bookkeeper for theft.

He was still out of the money!!

DEFENSE FROM THEFT UTILIZING SAVING ACCOUNTS

Be willing to say IN THE INITIAL INTERVIEW that you are willing to file police charges if there is money missing.

You would be surprised why many employers don't file charges:

- They don't have enough controls on their bookkeeping procedures to know when money is missing.
- They feel sorry for the employee and "don't want to keep them from feeding their children."
- They just don't want to take the time and expense that hearings, court dates, and follow-up take.
- They don't want the general world out there to know they were scammed.

LOOK at your money on a regular basis. If you have a savings account, watch it like a hawk. If it is a business savings account or money market, it should be on your balance sheet and reconciled just like your operations account by the 15th of each month.

Do NOT let a bookkeeper have access to your private accounts no matter what.

THEFT THROUGH PAYROLL

I have seen all these done by pickpocket bookkeepers. These always include collusion with another person.

These errors and frauds bleed over to forms called 941 (IRS), 940 (IRS), and whatever form the State requires each quarter for the purposes of unemployment. All the government reports must match in information. Once these government forms are filed, it is **VERY** difficult to get them changed, and you will spend a LOT of time reconciling them.

Payroll is not for the faint-hearted or unskilled. If payroll is being handled in-house, I highly recommend the owner have a third-party accountant review all reports periodically.

24. Ghost Employees

The bookkeeper writes a payroll check to a "ghost employee."

CASE STUDY – BELIEVE IT OR NOT, THIS IS A TRUE STORY

My most memorable experience with this was when a County Commissioner had babysitters and maids on the County payroll at $38,000 per year per employee, and none of them ever worked a day in their lives at a county office. The employees split the money with the Commissioner, who paid a mortgage on a home with part of the money.

The County Treasurer got wind of this after five years, and one payday required every single employee in the County (4,000 employees) to pick up their own paychecks personally with ID from the Treasurer's office. The "ghost" employees never showed up, and the County Treasurer opened a legal investigation.

They found that payday at that Commissioner's office was a big deal. The Commissioner would have the employees sign the backs of the checks, then the Commissioner would go to a paycheck cashing place (who was in on the scam), get cash for each paycheck, take her cut off the top, and immediately go and make a mortgage payment on a rental house she owned, in which, coincidentally, one of the "ghost" employees resided.

The FBI followed her through several months of these actions, and it worked until the County Treasurer required ID in order to pick up the paychecks.

It turned out the Commissioner had done things like use one of her friends' documentation for hiring one of the "ghost" employees because the employee was illegally in the US and didn't have her own documentation. The Commissioner was paying for her personal maid AND her personal nanny with the "ghost" employees.

The Commissioner was in jail for almost 3 years, and THEN the state sued her. She got probation for 10 years and restitution of several hundred thousand dollars.

I have seen bookkeepers add their children to payroll without authorization, and when the children were only 8 years old.

I have seen bookkeepers add their mothers as a cleaner/janitor, yet there would be a separate vendor being paid for cleaning. The mother was a complete "ghost" employee.

25. **Bookkeeper writes an extra check to an employee.**

The bookkeeper does a check incorrectly on purpose. The owner signs all the payroll checks in a stack. After the checks are signed, the bookkeeper then says, "Hey, you signed Joe's check, and I thought there was a problem with hours; what about that?" The owner says, "This is wrong" and hands the check back to the bookkeeper. The bookkeeper goes to the computer and processes a correct check. The owner doesn't notice that the first check was not voided. The pickpocket bookkeeper has Joe cash both checks and turn over the first net check cash back to the bookkeeper. The bookkeeper pays the payroll taxes on both checks, all the reports balance, and does this three or four times a year, with the bookkeeper having a second unauthorized income.

26. Bookkeeper writes a final check to an employee who is no longer employed by the company.

The bookkeeper writes a small check as a final check to an employee that was owed no final check. The check is put into the middle of a stack of checks; the bookkeeper explains that the employee turned in a few hours for the final check, and the owner signs the check. In this scenario, the bookkeeper thief forged the endorsement on the back of the check and somehow got the multiple small checks processed into her account.

27. Bookkeeper and another employee collude to share an unauthorized raise.

The bookkeeper and another employee collude to split additional funds from an unauthorized raise given to the employee. This works where there are many employees and the owner is no longer in touch with how much each employee makes, especially when salaries are similar ($15.00, $15.25, $15.50 per hour). This would sound like a small amount of money, but think about it over a period of three years. Owners trust their bookkeepers to pay the correct rates.

28. The bookkeeper keeps raises allocated to other staff members.

This occurs when a key employee is handling Human Resources as well as the accounting system.

CASE STUDY

My client employed about 35 people. The company owner gave raises across the board, and the owner told the office manager/bookkeeper to handle it.

Instead, the office manager took all the raised amounts for herself and told staff that they can't get raises; the company isn't making enough. INSTEAD, the office manager told the staff she was such a good person she was going to make it up to them by authorizing extra vacation instead.

This pickpocket bookkeeper went from a salary of $35,000 per year to $105,000 per year, and no staff member complained, because they were getting three- and four-week vacations. They thought the doctor was just a nice guy to give them extra time off.

This went on for four years before someone accidentally said something to the doctor about "Thanks for the four weeks' vacation this year." At this point, the doctor called me for an audit of the payroll system, and I found out what the office manager had done. She was fired, and the staff couldn't believe what she had done – for years!! She was their FRIEND!!

29. Bogus reimbursements are made on paychecks.

The bookkeeper colludes with another employee for reimbursement of certain unapproved supplies/materials. The payroll system can be set up to allow for things like mileage, payback for supplies, etc. This means the gross payroll stays the same, but the NET check inflates. The bookkeeper and the other employee split the fraudulent amount.

30. This was BRILLIANT – Changing the payroll "buckets."

My hat is off to this human resource person. She had patience, brains, and really understood how all the payroll reporting to the government works.

I heard of this from a CPA who hired himself out as CEO for large companies, often with overseas operations where currency exchanges came into play.

(A "bucket" is a field that collects the total withheld from people's paychecks every time you run a check. At the end of the year, these "buckets" are used to create a W2.)

CASE STUDY

In every payroll program, there are "buckets" where each payroll that is processed adds up so reports at the end of the quarter and the end of the year can be calculated. These reports are Form 941 (Federal Income Tax, Social Security & Medicare), state unemployment reports, and Form 940 (the Federal Unemployment report). All these reports are generated from the payroll program and must match exactly.

In every payroll program, employees in large companies are passworded out; there are always two or three trusted individuals that have access to every one of these "bucket" fields. This is to make sure untrusted and/or unskilled workers cannot change the "buckets," and the reports remain in sync.

This company had about 200 employees. Payroll was every two weeks.

For his own personal bookkeeping records, the CPA put his paycheck into his own home accounting program. After four or five checks, he noticed that the year-to-date buckets didn't match what was on his check stub. It's very lucky the CPA had a payroll system at home and that he actually reconciled the numbers to notice the difference. KUDOS to the CPA!!

The CPA went to the HR manager and the company quietly investigated.

They found that the senior payroll processor, for YEARS, had been changing the year-to-date "buckets" on other employees, $1.00 here, $5.00 there, and adding the exact same amounts to HER "buckets," only with income tax withheld from her peers' and friends' checks—$ 100.00 out and $100.00 back into the buckets.

The effect was that all the payroll reports would still balance out for quarterly reports and for W-2's at the end of the year. The only thing was the employees would have XXXX money taken out of their checks, and MINUS-XXXX was being reported to the government. They lost money every time they got their payroll check because at the end of the year they would owe an amount of income tax. They were robbed by their co-worker.

The senior payroll employee was willing to wait until tax reporting time to get her money, when she received a giant refund back from the IRS for overpayment of HER Federal Income Tax. The overpayment was the amount she had stolen from her co-workers.

This went on for YEARS, and no one figured it out. There is really no estimate for how much the employee stole from her friends. Since the theft went on for so many years, the IRS regulations had changed many times, and there really was no way to calculate the loss.

DEFENSE FROM THEFT THROUGH PAYROLL

The defense for all these scenarios is to analyze the payroll reports. Each payroll generates what is called a Payroll Summary by Employee. As the owner and the person responsible for payroll, check the amounts and line items on the reports. These reports must be pulled directly from the authorized payroll system and not be on an Excel spreadsheet.

- Know what each employee makes per hour or month. If you are a small company, that is possible. If you are a larger company, have some sort of report provided to you regularly.
- If there is a reimbursement on any check, insist that the paid receipt be attached for review when checks are signed.
- It is Best Practice to have a third-party payroll service company do your payroll. Use direct deposit for the employee checks.
- If it is not possible to hire a third-party payroll service, be sure to get the Payroll Summary and the Payroll Detail report. All payroll checks should be direct deposited.

- Look for duplicated dates; be sure the numbers match what goes on the 941 and C-3 forms.
- When you get the current quarter's reports, get the last two quarters' reports also, and look to see if the numbers are similar. This will give you trends.
- For the situation with the "buckets" being changed, the solution to this problem is very complicated and almost impossible to ferret out. The best advice is to compare the payroll checks from a month prior for the amounts of taxes withdrawn from employees' checks and compare these amounts to your current reports. Manually add up each of the intervening payroll "buckets" and compare the total as it should be to the total as it appears on the current paycheck. If you find a discrepancy, you should call your CPA or another trusted bookkeeping contractor to perform a full and private forensic audit. **DO NOT TELL** your bookkeeper about the audit until the results are back from the contractor.

THEFT THROUGH GENERALLY SNEAKY ACCOUNTING

These issues are lumped together because they are single-issue theft situations I have seen at one time or another in the last 45 years.

31. Transfers Between Multiple Bank Accounts and/or Multiple Companies

It is common for small business owners to move money from one company to another. This is acceptable as long as at the end of the year the transfers receivable/payable between companies are reconciled for tax purposes. The CPA will need clear records in order to record transfers in each company.

Sometimes there are transfers to a company owner's personal bank account and back. No problem, it is all their money, and the CPA at the end of the year may or may not pick up a problem when the CPA does a reconciliation for tax purposes. I've seen it.

Unwary business owners may give bookkeepers transfer rights at their bank for ease of management. The bookkeeper tells the owner they are making sure there is enough money in each account to plan for vendor payments each week.

The pickpocket bookkeeper will transfer money multiple times, creating chaos in the system. It goes like this:

Transfer money from Company A, Bank Account A

Received money into Company A, Bank Account B, same amount.

Transfer money from Company A, Bank Account B, different amount

Receive money into Company B, Bank Account A, same amount.

Transfer money from Company B, Bank Account A, different amount

Receive money in Company B, Bank Account B, different amount.

Transfer the money from Company B, Bank Account B

Receive the money into the bookkeeper's bank account.

There is no deposit in any company bank account after that.

Some of the money is now in the thief's account.

Perform this process twenty-five times over a corporate year, and the time it takes to reconcile between companies and various bank accounts is excessive and may not even be done. These transfers are hard for a business owner to track because they are usually in different databases, not in one combined place. They are certainly on different bank statements.

DEFENSE FROM TRANSFERS BETWEEN MULTIPLE BANK ACCOUNTS and/or MULTIPLE COMPANIES

Require a monthly report from the bookkeeper (printed from the computer, not an Excel spreadsheet, or any other digital medium) that shows the details of the transfers.

Check the bank reconciliation reports for unresolved entries.

32. Property Insurance Claims

This scenario happened to one of my clients, with respect to an insurance claim.

CASE STUDY

The partners authorized a claim of $XXX; the bookkeeper filed a claim $56,000 more than authorized. The bookkeeper told each partner the other partner had approved the claim for the increased amount.

The insurance company paid the full claim, including the overage; the bookkeeper took the check to the bank to deposit and moved the $56,000 into her own bank account. She just wrote herself a check, then later deleted the check from the bookkeeping system. Then she recorded the deposit at the lower amount. The owners were only expecting the lower amount and never thought anything was wrong. When one owner asked about the $56,000, he was told the insurance company had not authorized the increase.

When the company's insurance rate went up at the next renewal date, the owner personally called the insurance carrier. This is when the paid claim amount came to light.

Up until that time, the company partners had no idea of the amount of the claim; they had trusted the bookkeeper to file it honestly, and both had thought the other partner was handling the details. The bookkeeper claimed she had received approval for the increased claim from the absent partner, and this worked until the company owner just asked, "Well, where is the $56,000?" Everything came to a screeching halt. They fired the bookkeeper.

In the case above, the insurance company actually prosecuted the bookkeeper, not the company owner. However, the bookkeeper had disappeared from sight. The owner's insurance policy was canceled (no reason was given), which was bad enough – getting new insurance was tough.

DEFENSE FROM PROPERTY INSURANCE CLAIMS

- Do NOT assume the bookkeeper is being truthful. Do not authorize the charge or check until you have spoken with the partner in question.
- Have regular partnership meetings and put these items under housekeeping at every meeting.
- If you can't get along with your partner, get a new partner. Warring partners never succeed in small business together. And this just gives an opening to a pickpocket bookkeeper.
- Keep Minutes of the corporate meetings and Corporate Resolutions in a three-ring binder named "Minutes Book," even if the notes are handwritten. This can be a defense if an entity like an insurance company approaches the company owner for a fraudulent insurance claim.

33. Additional Insurance Benefits Added to Insurance Policy Without Owner Knowledge

CASE STUDY

I recently worked with a company that had a 10-year bookkeeper leave the job. After she left, the new bookkeeper needed some training.

I started digging in, and the first thing I found was that the prior person had added all kinds of insurance benefits to the company-paid policy that the owner didn't know: dental insurance, vision insurance, lower deductible, added prescription coverage.

It added up to about $250 per month PER EMPLOYEE. The bookkeeper did not tell the other employees that the benefits were available, so she was the only one who actually took advantage of the additions.

The bookkeeper told the owner that the basic cost of insurance was just going up. He trusted her. For years, she had the greatest insurance benefits known to man!!

DEFENSE FROM ADDITIONAL INSURANCE BENEFITS ADDED TO POLICY

LOOK at the policy before you sign it. Talk to the insurance agent, and ask the question: "What have we added this year?"

34. Arranging for Increased Bonus/Commission

One of the worst management decisions regarding bonuses or commission is to agree to pay any kind of bonus/commission based on profit on the Profit and Loss Statement. This report can be manipulated by a smart bookkeeper, and I've seen it done recently.

Everything is date-based in a bookkeeping system. If a key employee (office administrator; office administrator who goes into collusion with another key employee) is paid based on the Profit and Loss, all the person has to do is change the dates for some of the expenses to either a prior date or a future date just long enough to get a printout on which to base commissions. There is not a great way for an owner of a company to defend against this fraud, and the information can fall through the cracks pretty fast.

For example: One single purchase of material/product made in December can be dated in February just long enough to get commission paid, then the date moved back to December at a later date to match the purchase records. OR, more commonly, instead of using the current year, the bookkeeper would use a prior year just long enough to get a printout.

CASE STUDY

I had a client who was an electrical engineering firm. They employed about 25 electricians and an office person.

I was given the accounting contract AFTER the in-house office person (bookkeeper) had quit the job and disappeared, leaving the job at the end of January.

The first thing I noticed was the tax return in no way reflected what was in the internal accounting system.

When I inquired with the tax return contractor, he faxed me a series of Excel spreadsheets that were provided to him for the purposes of preparing the last five years' tax returns.

These spreadsheets were in no way similar to the accounting systems.

The second thing I noticed was the payroll taxes were only partially paid – and by "partially" I mean the accounting system showed the company owed about $75,000 in payroll taxes. That would not include penalties and interest.

It turned out the bookkeeper was paid a very generous bonus ($15,000 + because the P&L looked so good). The bonus was calculated based on the Profit & Loss reports at the end of every year, payable by the 15th of January each year.

In order to get her bonus on the first of January, the bookkeeper was posting a check in the accounting system for the payroll taxes, which showed on the balance sheet the payroll taxes were lowered by the payments. The ONLY PROBLEM was the checks (ACH's, transfers, etc) were NOT RECONCILED. The payments are never actually processed through the bank.

This led the business owner to think he had lots of cash, all the liabilities were paid, he owed no one, and VOILA – GREAT BONUS.

The company owner was, in fact, liable for the payroll taxes. We hired a specialty firm to negotiate with the IRS to get some of the penalties and/or interest discounted, but the IRS is very specific about collecting payroll taxes. It took the business owner three years to pay off the IRS, and it greatly affected the amount he could take out of the business for his own family for those three years.

The bookkeeper disappeared. There was no recourse for the business owner.

DEFENSE FROM ARRANGING FOR INCREASED BONUS/COMMISSION

Bottom line: Pay commissions and bonuses based on other production metrics or hire a forensic accountant to review your bookkeeping system before you pay commissions.

35. "Divide and Conquer" and Keep Going

This scenario is really effective when one of the partners is remote or out of the office most of the time. This is also effective when the partners are at war, just like between divorced/divorcing parents with children.

When a pickpocket bookkeeper wants to process a questionable vendor payment, and there are multiple partners, the bookkeeper says things like, "Oh, I checked that with the partner." "I gave that to your partner." "Your partner asked for that." This could be either a straight-up vendor payment, or a reimbursement check, or a credit card charge.
A great analogy here would be a teenager pitting the parents against each other.

This is also common when the bookkeeper thief wants an extra check for reimbursements for something that was not an authorized expense.

DEFENSE FROM "DIVIDE AND CONQUER" AND KEEP GOING

As a partner, insist on monthly meetings with your partner to go over the RECONCILED reports, as discussed above. As a partner, at least you can spot the behavior early and be prepared to make financial changes.

The hired bookkeeper in a family business cannot say to any partner, "You can't write that check." The bookkeeper can only provide reports to both partners.

Where the bookkeeper becomes involved with this is when reports are not given to all partners in a timely manner (by the 15th of each calendar month). Sometimes the bookkeeper is in collusion with a family member or one of the partners, receiving an actual kickback. Sometimes the bookkeeper is involved personally with the family members. Sometimes the bookkeeper just makes a bad decision and protects the family member, maybe because that person is "having a hard time."

In either case, the bookkeeper is hired by ALL the partners and investors in the business and is ethically required to provide complete reports to all.

As a final word, there is one more topic not counted in the **“36 Ways Your Bookkeeper Steals From You.”** The reason it’s not counted is that it’s not a specific and identifiable process. It’s more a statement from someone who has done lots of bad bookkeeping. This is a hidden cost to companies, and it’s the situation that costs companies the most money in the long run.

BONUS TOPIC

JUST PLAIN BAD BOOKKEEPING

Surprisingly, the most wasted money I see with bookkeeping is my fees to go in and fix just plain bad bookkeeping.

I'm almost always referred to clients by a number of CPAs who have said to their clients, "Get a good bookkeeper or I won't do your taxes." Or I'm referred by a client that I have straightened out from really bad bookkeeping.

I'm not exorbitant, but I'm not cheap. Neither is anyone with my experience and skill level.

A. External Issues

What happens when the CPA gets your file for tax preparation? You pay a CPA $250 to $350 an hour for tax return filing. If the CPA starts working on the data and figures out that LOTS of postings are incorrect (income posted to expenses, assets posted to expenses), the CPA has to put together something called a "Working Trial Balance" and will do entries to move things around. This can be quick, or this can take a lot of time.

Which bill would you rather pay? A bill to a forensic accountant for two hours' work, or a bill for a CPA for 12 hours' work?

If you go to the bank for a loan, the review committee knows how the reports should look. They also have standard national statistics they use to compare them to your company statistics. If they get reports that don't make any sense, do you think you will get that Line of Credit?

B. Internal Issues

Most importantly, you need to know if you are making money!! Cash flow and profit are two different issues. Without accurate reports, you could be in for an unpleasant surprise sometime in the future.

As a business owner, you are supporting yourself, your family, and who knows how many more people. If you aren't making money, you need to know this so you can make the hard decisions.

Business ownership is HARD.

I recently had a client ask, "How am I supposed to know all these reporting agencies? How does a small businessperson get educated in all this stuff so they can stay afloat?"

My answer: "Find a really good consultant bookkeeper/business consultant to help you through it." This means someone who understands the daily postings, the payroll compliance, and other compliance issues that you as the business owner have obligated yourself to by virtue of being the person in charge.

The accounting books you keep are only useful to you if they give you meaningful reports. Otherwise, doing all the paperwork and paying for a bookkeeper is just a waste of time and money. You might as well not do it. You can only hope you stay off the IRS's radar forever, because once you are audited for one year, you stand a good chance of being monitored for years to come.

Good bookkeeping gives you management tools at your fingertips.

At first, owners can't stand me, because I'm like an irritating barking dog –

- "I need this information; I'm not through yet. Where is this? Get me that."
- "No, I'm not through yet. Be patient. And what is this that I have found?"

Then later, I can say things like:

- Did you know you paid your computer guy $15,000 this year? What for? The contract I saw would have been about $7,000."
- **Or** "Why is your maintenance man charging twice for the same thing? Look at the data."
- **Or** "Did you know you have four customers that owe you for work you did six months ago? When exactly do you do your collections? Your

bookkeeper said you told her not to collect these accounts. Is she special friends with them?"

- **Or** "I have found checks in your system that have one vendor name, and there is another vendor on the actual check. What's going on?"
- **Or** "Did you know you gave your bookkeeper a $5.00 per hour raise two years ago and she authorized additional insurance for your whole company last year?"

Business is run on statistics. Follow the statistics, and you make money! Stop looking at your statistics, and your company may be <u>shut down in a couple of years</u>, and you will be looking for a job.

Most owners can do their core work really well – that's why they go into business in the first place. However, the infrastructure of business management is foreign to them. It's hard to learn, and it's costly if it's messed up.

Get smart.

Ask for help from your CPA – get them to refer someone; they may know good bookkeepers, not necessarily working internally in the CPA firm, which can be pricey. If you can't get a referral there, go to your biggest client, ask them who they use. Go to your bookkeeping software provider, see if they have certifications and have a list of certified bookkeepers you can interview.

Suppose you need to hire someone full-time; interview carefully. ALWAYS get references and be sure you know with whom you are speaking. I have actually gone to a referencing business personally and met with the ex-boss for a face-to-face referral. It is crucial when you are searching for someone to manage anything that has to do with your money.

UPDATE: MAY 2026

As I was editing this document, I attended two local networking meetings. There was a total of approximately 30 people combined at the meetings.

In these two networking events, I met **TWO** business owners who had experienced **THREE** thefts by bookkeepers.

One of the business owners had a small side business where the bartender was converting sale tickets to complimentary tickets when the patron paid cash for the ticket. This was not too bad, only about $4,000 dollars in six months. The owner of the company did not prosecute the employee.

However, that same business owner also owned a large corporation. The CFO of the corporation had embezzled $400,000. The CFO managed the cash assets of the company and misappropriated funds somehow. The owner prosecuted the person, who went to jail for seven years.

The other person I met found that her trusted companion in business, the office manager/bookkeeper, had taken over $20,000 in three years. This business owner was devastated by the betrayal of the key employee. However, the business owner did not prosecute – because they had been such good friends.

My point is: In ONE week, purely by accident, I ran across three more incidents of Pickpocket Bookkeepers, and one of the situations was very serious.

CLOSING THOUGHTS

DISCLAIMER:

This document is strictly from the standpoint of the employer with regard to theft from a key employee who has access to the company's monetary systems. Other human resource issues are ignored. While I also have quite a bit of experience in human resource management, and I do not intentionally include any recommendation that might be construed to conflict with any employment regulation from any entity (and there are many), this is a disclaimer that each employer will have to adjust their own internal systems to remain in compliance with human resource regulations.

For the purposes of this limited discussion, I'm going to state: The **ONLY** thing that matters to you as an owner is that you are earning money, and that the money makes it to **YOUR** bank account and stays there until **YOU** decide to spend it.

This document is also very straightforward and direct, and I pull no punches.

There is a saying in business management:

IT IS NOT ALWAYS THE MONEY YOU MAKE –

IT IS THE MONEY YOU KEEP.

This is mostly referring to spending unnecessarily and unwisely, or not managing the company cash flow to accommodate lean times. However, it speaks directly to being the type of company owners/managers who do not educate themselves or pay enough attention to the internal operations of a company in order to allow the above scenarios to play out.

While it is true that a pickpocket bookkeeper (or financial manager) of a company can successfully hide cash drain for a period of time, eventually there are warning signs that will pop up. It's the company managers who ignore the warning signs who expose their company to theft of larger sums of cash.

Thanks for your time. This has been a labor of love across many years. I wish you well.

– Charlie Montgomery

YOUR NEXT STEPS

As separate topics, you may need the information in two additional educational guides:

1. **"How To Hire a Bookkeeper."**
   Some of the topics in that document are:
   - General Interviewing Rules
   - There are gypsies among us!!
   - Job Description Suggestions
   - Interviewing Questions with Answers

   If you haven't had success in the past hiring a bookkeeper, this tutorial will provide the language needed to gauge the level of skill of the person you are considering for your company.

   This information can be what is standing between you and a disastrous hiring decision.

2. **What is The Blueprint for a Successful Pickpocket Bookkeeper?**

   There you will find:

   - How does a scenario get set up so a trusted employee has access to cash anyway?
   - The basic blueprint for Pickpocket Bookkeepers.
   - What are the signs you might be in trouble?
   - What happens when a company owner suspects and even proves theft?
   - What are some basic preventative steps you can take to protect yourself?

These two documents are loaded with excellent information every business owner needs in order to hire and manage the bookkeeper in their company successfully.

CONVICTIONS FROM THE IRS

IRS has a Press Release website.

IRS.GOV/compliance/criminal-investigation

Practically every month, there is an article regarding accounting or bookkeeper fraud.

Just for fun, I've taken a couple of these articles and posted a summary.

What you will never see is small amounts with the IRS. They only process the largest thefts. Small businesses never make it into this cycle.

1. According to court documents, Alicia Henderson was the office manager and bookkeeper for a non-profit corporation that provided services for the San Antonio Downtown Public Improvement District. Her responsibilities included oversight of the accounting and financial reporting functions for the non-profit corporation.
   Between July 2014 and November 2017, Alicia Henderson forged or wrote 118 checks drawn on the non-profit's bank account and deposited the funds in her personal bank account. She stole $291,385.23 for her personal benefit and failed to report the embezzled funds on her taxes. Alicia Henderson owed $64,719 in taxes for 2014 to 2016.
   The courts sentenced Alicia Henderson to 33 months in prison for financial and tax fraud, as well as restitution of $356,104.23.

2. In Wichita, Kansas, Nancy Martin worked for Mid-Kansas Wound Specialists and Emergency Services P.A. as a bookkeeper, business manager, and chief operating officer.
   During that time, from 2012 to 2017, she embezzled $3.1 million by fraudulently obtaining money from her employer's banks. But that wasn't all. Also, during that time, specifically from 2013 to 2016, she either filed tax returns or caused tax returns to be filed with the IRS that omitted income, causing a tax loss of about $670,000.

3. Take the case of Kimberly Sue Peterson-Janovec. Not only was she caught embezzling from the company that she worked for, but she has been caught 3 times!!
   Starting in 1998, Kimberly Sue Peterson-Janovec was convicted of embezzling \$950,000 from her employer. Then, from 2014 to 2019, she took over \$881,000 from MI5 and the Denny's Corporation in bogus vendor payments, fraudulent payroll submissions, and cash deposits. After discovering aspects of her fraud, MI5 terminated her employment. Not to be discouraged, Kimberly Sue Peterson-Janovec then lied about her work experience and got a job for Company 3, a construction company in Rochester; she managed to get another \$350,000 in as little as 18 months!!
   On February 22, 2022, Peterson-Janovec was convicted by a federal jury on 24 counts of fraud, aggravated identity theft, and tax crimes.

4. In Indianapolis, Indiana, Jody Russell Trapp was finally sentenced to 90 months in Federal Prison for wire fraud, money laundering, and tax evasion.
   Jody Russell Trapp worked for Shelton Machinery, Inc from July 2009 to December 2011 as a bookkeeper, overseeing the preparation and mailing of checks to outside vendors. During that time, he stole more than \$2.2 million from the company by diverting checks to his personal account. He did this by preparing fictitious or duplicate invoices for work that had already been billed and paid, as well as checks to pay the fictitious or duplicate invoices. Jody Russell Trapp was arrested in January 2012 and charged in June of the same year. After
   changing his plea and pushing back his court date into March of 2013, he disappeared two weeks before his court hearing.
   Eight years later, in October of 2021, he was finally located and arrested, living under an assumed name in Utah. U.S. Marshals escorted Jody Russell Trapp back to Indiana, and he pleaded guilty on July 19th, 2022.